SCIENTIFIC GOOFS

ADVENTURES
ALONG THE
CROOKED
TRAIL
TO TRUTH

SCIENTIFIC GOOFS

ADVENTURES ALONG THE CROOKED TRAIL TO TRUTH

BILLY ARONSON

ILLUSTRATED BY LYNN BRUNELLE

Scientific American
BOOKS FOR YOUNG READERS

W. H. Freeman and Company
New York

Text copyright © 1994 by Billy Aronson
Illustrations copyright © 1994 by Lynn Brunelle
All rights reserved. No part of this book may be reproduced by any mechanical, photographic, or electronic process, or in the form of a phonographic recording, nor may it be stored in a retrieval system, transmitted, or otherwise copied for public or private use, without the written permission of the publisher.

Book design by Marsha Cohen/Parallelogram Graphics

Library of Congress Cataloging-in-Publication Data

Aronson, Billy.
Scientific Goofs: Adventures Along the Crooked Trail to Truth/ Billy Aronson.
p. cm.
Includes index.
ISBN 0-7167-6537-3 (hardcover)
ISBN 0-7167-6553-5 (paperback)
1. Serendipity in science—Juvenile literature.
2. Research—Methodology—Juvenile literature. [1. Discoveries in science. 2. Science—Methodology.] I. Title.
Q172.5.S47A76 1994
507.2—dc20   94-4492
                    CIP
                    AC

Printed in the United States of America
10 9 8 7 6 5 4 3 2 1

To Nancy Laties Feresten, an editor who's brilliant, imaginative, brave, tactful—and has a sense of humor! What more could any writer want?

And to my wife, Lisa Vogel, who inspires my goofs, endures my spoofs, and shares my roofs.

Contents

The Goof
Is in the Pudding

All of a sudden you find yourself floating through space on a gigantic rock that's covered with blobs. Questions rush through your mind. "How did I get here? Where did these blobs come from? Where did this rock come from? Where's the rock going?" But the one question you need to deal with before all the others is, "What's for dinner?"

So you take a risk. You bite into a little red blob. It tastes disgusting, so you spit it out. You bite a big blue blob. Yuck! Even worse. Then you bite a yellow blob. Not bad! You bite another yellow blob. Yum! After biting three more yellow blobs, you come to an important conclusion: Yellow blobs are delicious— bite away! So you bite another yellow blob, and another. Then you bite a large yellow blob. It bites you back. It knocks you down. It stomps on your belly, rubs its fur all over your face, and prances away. You goofed!

But the goof you goofed is a special kind of goof. It's different from mindless goofs, like falling out of bed or stepping on a piece of gum or forgetting to put your pants on and showing up at a party in your underwear. Unlike those goofs, the blob-biting goof is a scientific goof.

Why is choosing which blob to bite scientific? Because science is simply the way we try to understand or control nature. (Nature here doesn't mean just trees, grass, and daffodils. It means everything on Earth, and in the rest of the universe.) Whenever we try to figure out the world around us, we're on a scientific journey that we hope will lead to the truth.

Science books are full of scientific truths. Scientists combined knowledge, courage, patience, and good hunches to come up with these truths. But science books don't usually say much about scientific goofs. To come up with certain goofs, scientists also combined knowledge, courage, patience, and good hunches. So what's the difference? To the truths we say "Aha!" and to the goofs we say "Ha ha!"

Yes, scientific goofs are funny. But they're also important. Think about the goof with the blobs. The rule that yellow blobs should be bitten seemed to make good sense. It was tested, and it held up for a little while. Then it proved to be hilariously wrong. It led to a blunder as looney as any cartoon! But it paved the way for progress, too—leading to the discovery of live creatures on the rock!

The process by which our primitive ancestors made such crucial discoveries as fire, fur, and farming probably involved scientific goofs of this kind. And since prehistoric times, many of our most laughable goofs have led to our most valuable scientific truths.

So let's celebrate the goofs—the most stupendous, glorious, courageous, comical goofs in the history of science! This book pays tribute to some of the great goofs that have given us so much to learn from, and to laugh at.

How come it's okay to laugh at the goofs when we're supposed to be honoring them? Because when we laugh at the goofs, we're also laughing at ourselves. We're laughing at our brave, urgent, hilarious struggle to under-stand the weird rock on which we're floating through space.

So let
the goofs
begoon!

What's Up?

D o you ever look up at the sky and scream in horror? There's a big yellow circle up there that's in a different place every time you check. Suddenly the circle sinks and disappears completely, and a thousand sparkling dots appear. What's going on up there?

Chances are you never panic when you look at the sky. You know what those bright shapes are. You know that though they look small and close, the sun, moon, and stars are really huge and far away. But you didn't get this information on your own. Scientists have been studying the sky for thousands of years, often with the help of complicated scientific instruments, to learn what we now know about the universe.

But for the sake of experiment, forget everything you already know about those shapes in the sky. Then study them using nothing but the same kind of built-in instruments ancient astronomers relied on: your own

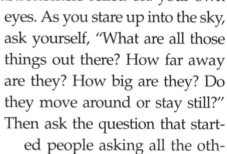

eyes. As you stare up into the sky, ask yourself, "What are all those things out there? How far away are they? How big are they? Do they move around or stay still?" Then ask the question that started people asking all the others: "How do I fit in to all this?"

If you get the feeling you're at the center of everything, you're not the first. From ancient times until relatively recently, people thought Earth was the center of the universe

6

and that everything else revolved around it.

One reason people believed this idea was that observations supported it. The sun does look like it's moving around Earth as it rises in the east, crosses overhead, then sets in the west. And Earth definitely doesn't feel like it's moving around beneath your feet (unless you live in California!).

Another reason people believed Earth was the center of everything is because we're conceited. It's easy for us to convince ourselves that where we live is the center of all the action and excitement, the most important place to be.

But an important reason the idea was believed so widely for so long is because of the work of one man: a scientist called Ptolemy, who lived in the Roman Empire.

Like many thinkers whose ideas spread far and wide, Ptolemy had the good fortune to be working in the right place at the right time. In his case, it was Alexandria, Egypt, in the second century. Though Rome was the official capital of the vast Roman Empire, Alexandria was the place all the great scholars and scientists of the day came to work and share ideas—as they come to cities like New York or Paris today. In this exciting town on the northern coast of Africa, Ptolemy developed a detailed picture of how the Earth-centered universe worked, and came up with some scientific reasoning to support it.

One thing that impressed Ptolemy was the result of a very simple experiment you can try anytime: dropping a rock. When you let go of a rock, it doesn't float away but falls to Earth. This reminded Ptolemy of the way the sun, moon, planets, and stars don't just float away from Earth, but keep on coming back, day after day.

Ptolemy figured that things on Earth and in the sky should follow the same rules. Since a rock's movement is centered on Earth, the movement of objects in the sky must also be centered on Earth.

For Ptolemy, these facts proved that Earth sits still, smack in the middle of everything, as the moon, the sun, the planets, and all the stars swirl around it.

To put together an accurate picture of the universe, Ptolemy kept records of the movements of Mars, Saturn, Jupiter, Venus, and Mercury (all the planets known at the time), and of over a thousand stars. The stars moved the way Ptolemy expected them to; they seemed to be circling Earth. But sometimes the planets didn't appear to move in perfect circles. So Ptolemy decided that as the planets move along their big circles, they must also swirl around in little cycles called "epicycles."

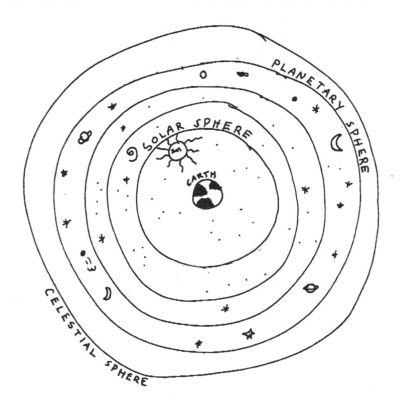

Ptolemy's work spread from Alexandria throughout the Roman Empire. It was translated into Arabic and spread across the Middle East. There it was embraced by Muslims, who referred to the book containing Ptolemy's ideas simply as "The Greatest." It was embraced by Christians, too, and was spread across Europe by priests and poets alike for a thousand years. People all over the world were drawn to this picture that matched astronomers' observations so well, was so beautifully simple, and put human beings at the center of everything.

As scientists got better at studying the sky, they noticed that the planets seemed to move in ways Ptolemy hadn't noticed. But rather than throw out Ptolemy's picture, they adjusted his paths, adding all kinds of squiggles, blips, and twists. Scientists bent over backward to preserve Ptolemy's picture!

Finally, in the 1400s, a Polish man named Copernicus saw a way to explain the movements in the sky without adding squiggles—but to do it, he had to disagree with Ptolemy and draw a whole new picture.

Disagreeing with Ptolemy was a startling thing to do. But Copernicus lived in an age called the Renaissance, when people all across Europe were questioning beliefs that had been accepted as truths for centuries, and coming up with startling new ideas. Like many great thinkers of the day, Copernicus was skilled in several different fields. Though he earned his living keeping accounts for a church, his work left him time to study everything from medicine to law to math to painting, and to pursue his hobby of astronomy.

While studying the stars, Copernicus was struck by an idea. Instead of adding more and more complicated changes to Ptolemy's picture, putting in one single change could make the picture much simpler. What if the sun and the planets didn't revolve around Earth? What if Earth and the planets revolved around the sun? Copernicus pointed out that though the sun looks like it's moving, it could be staying completely still as Earth moves. In other words, when the sun looks like it's going down, it might really be that Earth is going up!

The idea that Earth wasn't the center of everything made people furious. How dare Copernicus say that Earth is just one of a bunch of puny planets circling the grand sun! How dare he make the people who live on Earth sound so unimportant in the scheme of things! But only a few decades after Copernicus's death, scientists pointed their newly invented telescopes toward the sky and proved that Copernicus's suggestion was right. Their proof blew the roof off Ptolemy's goof.

Now, with satellite telescopes gathering facts from billions and billions of miles away, we know even more about our place in the universe. We know that Earth goes around the sun, as Copernicus suggested. But we also know something Copernicus didn't—that even our grand sun isn't the center of the universe. It's just a rather small star among the billions of stars that make up the Milky Way Galaxy. And the Milky Way isn't the center of everything either. It's one of countless clusters of galaxies floating through a universe that might be boundless. Compared to the rest of the universe, our beloved planet is a tiny speck of cosmic dust. The universe doesn't exactly revolve around us after all, does it!

So Ptolemy goofed. But by looking at the universe scientifically, he came up with a picture that included many of the elements our present picture has. We still see the universe as an arrangement of planets and stars, moved around by the same force—gravity— that moves objects toward the ground. And remember, it was only by encountering Ptolemy's picture—worshiping it, then using Ptolemy's own method of careful observation to challenge it, and finally putting it aside—that we arrived at our own. Among glorious goofs, Ptolemy's really was "The Greatest."

Good as Gold

One day about six thousand years ago, a gang of cave people got sick of having to make everything out of sticks, stones, and the metals that they dug out of the ground. Their tin cups were getting rusty. Their copper-tipped spears were bending. So they melted tin and copper and mixed them together, to make a new metal we now call bronze. When these cave people brought bronze cups to their lips, the rims weren't rusty. When they stabbed enemies with bronze-tipped spears, the tips didn't bend. Life was great!

You can mix materials to improve your life too. Take a glass of milk and mix in a teaspoon of sugar and a teaspoon of chocolate powder. Chances are you're happy with the change—everybody likes chocolate milk!

Since prehistoric times, there's one thing people have craved more than bronze or chocolate: gold. Maybe because it's so beautiful. Maybe because it's so rare. Maybe because it never rusts or blackens, but always stays bright and shiny. Whatever the reason, for a long time people thought gold was the perfect material—the best thing on Earth. They crossed continents, sailed seas, and marched off to war in their desperate search for gold.

But not everybody thought the best way to get gold was to risk your life for it. Some believed gold could be created by putting the right materials together. Alchemists, as they were called, devoted their lives to this quest. One of most devoted and brilliant of all the alchemists was a woman named Maria who lived in the second century in Alexandria (the same time and place Ptolemy was studying the stars).

Maria took the dream of making gold very seriously. She wasn't going to just slop a bunch of stuff together till she got lucky. Maria felt that creating this perfect material would take great care. She wanted to do her mixing in a series of very careful steps, controlling the temperature, the purity, and even the positions of the materials.

In those days, there were no tools for doing the type of careful mixing Maria wanted to do. But this didn't stop Maria—she invented her own tools!

To heat a liquid slowly and carefully, she invented the water bath. In a water bath you heat a pan of water, which in turn heats a small pot of liquid that sits in the pan. Nowadays we call this double-boiling. When your parents double-boil fudge topping to make it hot without burning it, they're using a method Maria invented almost two thousand years ago!

The main invention Maria used in her search for gold was the kerotakis. To use it, Maria put a piece of common metal, such as copper, lead, or tin, on a plate near the top. Then she put a liquid that she hoped would change this metal to gold in the bottom. When she heated the liquid, it turned to a vapor that rose up and brushed across the metal. As the vapor hit the dome, it

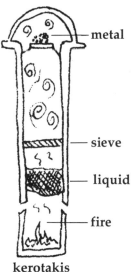

kerotakis

15

cooled, turned to liquid, dripped down, and was heated again . . . so the kerotakis would keep going and going till the job was done. And Maria felt certain the job would be done as soon as she found the right common metal and liquid.

Why was she so certain? Because of Maria's theory about materials. Maria believed that materials act like animals. Certain pairs of animals, like a dog and a donkey, won't have anything to do with each other. You put them together and they just sit there, or walk away, or fall asleep! But if you put a male dog and a female dog together, something happens. They get excited. They start jumping around. They get together! Maria felt that if she could find the perfect pair of materials, they'd go together in this way—and the result of their perfect pairing would be the perfect metal: gold.

When the liquid in her kerotakis was arsenic sulphide and the metal was a mixture of copper and lead, Maria seemed to have found her dogs! As the vapors hit the metal, it turned black. Then the black dripped away. Soon the metal turned golden! It didn't  turn to gold, but it did take on gold color. Maria took this as a clue that she was on the right track.

She tried other liquids that were like arsenic sulphide. She tried other metals that were like copper and lead. In many cases the metals turned golden. But they never turned to gold.

In the centuries that followed, news of Maria's work spread around the world. Others made use of her discoveries—but Maria wouldn't have been happy with the use they made of them. These alchemists spent more time trying to fool people into thinking they'd made gold than trying to really make it. They acted like magicians instead of scientists.

Why couldn't Maria make gold? The answer had to wait until the late 1600s. Though the Renaissance had ended by then, its spirit of curiosity lived on. All across Europe large universities sprang up where sci-

17

entists questioned old ideas and debated new ones. This questioning led to new theories, new break-throughs, and to a new field that explained exactly how and why things mix: modern chemistry. According to the laws of modern chemistry, you can't create gold by putting other materials together, because gold is an element.

Elements are like building blocks. They're the basic units that make up all matter. You can put a group of wooden blocks together to make a tower. You can rearrange the blocks to make a bridge. Or a castle. Or a tunnel. But no matter what you do with these blocks, you can't make a wooden block into a Lego!

And that's what Maria was trying to do. She didn't know that gold isn't a combination of different things, the way bronze and chocolate milk are, but a basic building block called an element. She didn't know that unless she was working with a material that already had gold in it, she would never end up with gold. Trying to create gold by mixing things was a goof.

Though Maria didn't find gold, her theory about how certain materials go together was right on the money. We still talk about elements as though they were living creatures—we group them into "fami-lies." And we know that when elements of certain families are put with elements of certain other fami-lies they give off bursts of smoke, heat, and light—

reacting as swiftly as male and female dogs.

More importantly, Maria's method of creating scientific setups and carefully putting materials together is still in use today. Modern scientists follow in Maria's footsteps as they put materials together to create everything from fabrics that make stronger clothes to medicines that save lives.

So hats off to Maria—for a goof as gold!

Where on Earth?

There must be a better route to your neighborhood swimming pool! You have to go left all the way around a train station, then right past a garbage dump, then right again through a marsh that's swarming with mosquitoes. You show up at the pool covered with mud, itching like crazy . . . and too exhausted to swim.

You're tempted to try a shortcut straight through a forest. But what's inside the forest? A steep mountain? A wide river? Or a path that leads straight to your house? One thing's certain: You'd feel better about this shortcut if you had a map!

Luckily for shortcut seekers everywhere, the whole world is mapped out. There are maps of every city, state, and nation on the planet.

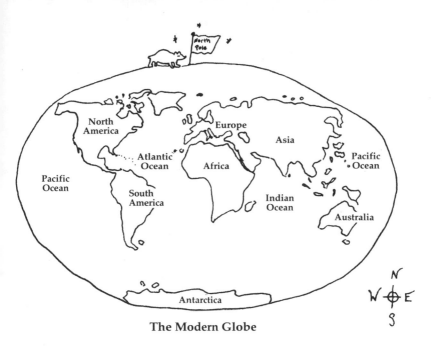

The Modern Globe

Check your nearest globe. Can you find any blank spots or question marks? No, the whole ball's filled in. The blue background of ocean is filled with scattered small splotches and two big blobs: a Europe-Asia-Africa blob, and a North-and-South-America blob.

But the globe wasn't always all filled in. Through most of history, people on each of the big blobs thought their blob was the only blob. Neither blob knew about the other!

And how should they have? The blobs are separated by huge oceans. Each blob has plenty of land. There was no reason for anyone from either blob to go blob-hopping. In fact, there was rarely any reason for anyone to go far from their own little section of their blob—until the 1400s.

In those days Europeans called their blob the Island of Earth, since they thought it was all the land there was. They thought their island was surrounded by the only ocean in the world, which they called the Ocean Sea.

To many Europeans, their island suddenly felt way too wide. They wanted to get to the Indies—China, Japan, and India—to trade for the precious gold and spices that were plentiful there.

To make the journey, Europeans had to sail from one sea to another to another to another. Then they had to make their way across miles and miles of land

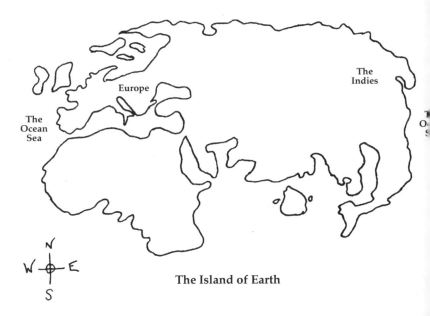

The Island of Earth

that was covered with enormous deserts and towering mountains. Plus, they had to deal with the Ottomans—members of an Asian empire that was often at war with Europeans.

But an Italian sailor named Christopher Columbus had an idea for a shortcut. Columbus felt sure that if he sailed west from Europe, he'd wind up on the other side of the world in a few short weeks.

Certain observations supported Columbus's theory. For one thing, Columbus had heard from other sailors that two corpses with oval-shaped eyes that made them appear Asian had floated ashore from the west.

But Columbus also believed the Indies weren't far for nonscientific reasons. Like many people of his time, he'd been taught that Earth was created for the good of people. Everything on Earth provided food, shelter, comfort, or enjoyment. So it just didn't make sense that half the world would be covered with ocean—and be of so little use to people! Since he thought the ocean took up a small part of the planet, Columbus figured getting across wouldn't take long.

Columbus felt sure he was right. But being sure wasn't enough. He still needed to convince someone rich—like a king or queen—to give him the ship and crew he'd need to make the journey.

So Columbus collected information from famous scientists to put together a package of evidence that would fit his beliefs.

When it came to the size of Earth, Columbus had plenty of answers to choose from. Scientists had been coming up with them for thousands of years. In ancient times the Greek Eratosthenes had tried to calculate the size of Earth by measuring how shadows change as the sun moves—and had come up with a number that we now know was almost exactly right! More recently, the Arab Alfragan had arrived at a larger number. But Alfragan's number was published in Arab miles instead of European miles. When Columbus converted Alfragan's number to European miles, he did the math wrong and got a very small number. Delighted with his goofed result—a small Earth—

Columbus used it to support his claims.

Columbus chose Paolo Toscanelli's map for the same reason: It confirmed what he already believed. Toscanelli thought Japan was farther east than other mapmakers did, so his map made it look closer to Europe. Columbus didn't want to listen to other thinkers of the day who claimed the ocean was way too big to cross, or even that it went on forever.

Columbus's geography was pretty sloppy by modern scientific standards, but it did convince at least one person: the queen of Spain. She gave him three ships, a crew to man them, and a note to deliver to the emperor of China.

Not long after they'd set sail, Columbus's crew began to wonder if the ocean didn't really go on forever! This was no quick trip. But Columbus wouldn't give up. He and his crew sailed on and on and on through the waves . . . never seeing a bird, a floating leaf, or any other trace of land . . . for two months! Then, one morning at sunrise, a member of Columbus's crew spotted land.

When they reached the shore, the Europeans were amazed to see people who were almost naked smoking a plant they'd never seen: tobacco. The natives were amazed to see people decked out in layers of heavy clothing even though it was a very hot day.

At a moment like this, scientists get right to work asking questions and studying details to see if their original theory was right. If new evidence proves the theory wrong, they revise it.

Hot enough for ya?

But Columbus wasn't interested in revising his theory. He was sure he'd reached the Indies, so he called the natives Indians. After sniffing some shrub that had a faint aroma, Columbus was sure it was the Chinese spice cinnamon. When the natives told him about a nearby land called Cuba, he was thrilled because he thought they meant China. When members of his crew doubted they were in Asia, Columbus got so mad he threatened to cut out their tongues.

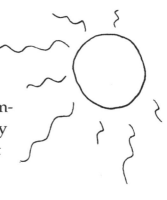

Adjusting observations to make them fit a theory is called fudging. Columbus didn't return to Europe with Asian spice, just a lot of Columbian fudge. Though many believed Columbus had made it to China, many had their doubts . . . including some other explorers, who decided to find out for themselves.

After Columbus's death, Ferdinand Magellan took his ships across the ocean to Columbus's "Indies," then onward to another ocean, and then all the way around the real Asia. This journey settled it: Columbus hadn't reached Asia, but another continent. Columbus had goofed.

But what a goof! Columbus had stumbled upon a huge blob that Europeans didn't even know was out there! Soon all the main pieces of the globe fell into place. South America. North America. The

Pacific. The Atlantic. Columbus's search for a shortcut to Asia by sailing west was a goof that led to an avalanche of understanding about our globe.

Now that Earth is all mapped, we look to space. Though we've sent satellites millions of miles into space, we have yet to find

life. So it's hard to imagine a space journey that would lead to as much shocking new knowledge as Columbus's sea journey did.

But who knows. Maybe someday, while on a routine cruise between planets, one of our space ships will bump into a huge floating blob that isn't on any of our maps. Maybe it will be inhabited by creatures whose culture, language, and maps of the universe are completely different from ours.

Or maybe someday a space creature will take a wrong turn and discover us!

Creepy Creation

Yeech! That piece of candy on your floor is completely covered with ants! The glop of peanut butter in your garbage can is crawling with worms! The (WE HIDE!) dead squirrel on the road is swarming with flies! How did all those disgusting little creatures get there?

For thousands of years people have wondered how little creatures can appear so suddenly in certain places. When you think about it, it's pretty weird.

Take that ant-covered piece of candy behind your bookshelf for example. You might not see any other ants in your room. Or anywhere else in the whole house! But the candy is teeming with them. How did so many of those little creatures end up in one place?

30

To explain these creepy creature crowds, people came up with the idea of spontaneous generation. If you spontaneously decide to do something, you make the decision suddenly, and you make it by yourself. Spontaneous generation occurs if an animal comes to life all of a sudden, without any other live animal playing a part. According to the theory of spontaneous generation, ants on candy come from the candy, worms in garbage come from bits of garbage, and flies swarming around a dead squirrel were spontaneously generated by the dead squirrel.

Over the years, people have supposed that all kinds of sudden, strange animal appearances were caused by spontaneous generation. Some people believed geese sprang to life from trees, or that lambs could come from melons. Some believed frogs in a puddle had been spontaneously generated by rain clouds and dropped to the ground with the rain.

Then, in the 1600s, someone decided to put spontaneous generation to the test. Belgian scientist Jean-Baptiste Van Helmont covered a heap of sweaty shirts with wheat and studied the heap to see if animals would appear. And they did! After 21 days Van Helmont found the shirts crawling with rats. From this he concluded that sweaty shirts and wheat give birth to rats.

Some scientists felt Van Helmont had made history. Others felt he'd made ha-story. As scientists created experiments to prove or disprove his results, a scientific tug-of-war began that would last for two hundred years.

German scientist Athanasius Kircher tried a different approach that led to the same conclusion. When he collected a bunch of dead flies and poured honey over them, live flies soon appeared, swarming around the dead ones. This convinced Kircher that dead flies and honey give birth to live flies.

But something about these experiments bothered Italian scientist Francesco Redi. To see if dead materials could really give birth to live animals, he gathered dead snakes, dead pigeons, veal chops, horse flesh, and the heart of a lamb. But unlike Van

Helmont and Kircher, Redi placed his materials in a covered box, to keep little animals from getting in.

Because Redi took the extra step of covering the materials, his can be called a controlled experiment. In a controlled experiment, a scientist makes sure only one part of the problem is tested at a time. Redi felt Van Helmont's experiment tested not one but two things at the same time: whether animals could be born from materials and whether animals could be lured to materials.

And Redi was right. His extra control led to different results: no rats, no flies, no worms. In fact, he found flies outside of the box trying to get in!

But with the invention of the microscope, scientists found new reasons to believe in spontaneous generation. When they peered through

DEAD THINGS

a microscope at a drop of water, scientists saw thousands of wiggly oval animals swimming around. These "animalcules" could also be found in the guts of frogs, in the feces of mice, and on teeth. How could they show up in such tiny, tucked-away places if not by spontaneous generation?

Englishman John Needham decided to see if spontaneous generation was in fact responsible for these wee weird wigglers. He heated vegetable juice to kill off any animalcules that might be there, then poured the juice into a test tube and let it sit. Soon Needham found more animalcules swimming around in the juice. Once again a test seemed to prove spontaneous generation.

And once again somebody didn't buy it. Italian scientist Lazzaro Spallanzani had a hunch Needham's animalcules came from outside the tube. So he heated vegetable juice and poured it into a test tube—but then sealed the tube tightly. Again a controlled experiment brought different results: no animalcules. Spallanzani announced that he'd disproved spontaneous generation.

But Needham wasn't impressed. He felt that by sealing the tube, Spallanzani had made it impossible for the animalcules that had sprung to life to breathe. According to Needham, in Spallanzani's tube there had been spontaneous generation . . . followed by spontaneous suffocation!

Then French scientist Louis Pasteur thought of a brilliant way to keep animalcules outside the tube from getting in— without suffocating any that might already be in there. Pasteur's experiment was like Needham's and Spallanzani's, but with one important difference: He put his vegetable juice into a flask that had a long, curved neck. This curved neck would let air in, so no one could accuse Pasteur of suffocating the animalcules. But it would also keep animalcules out, since its long, dipping curve was surely too steep for such tiny creatures to scale.

It's been *years!* Still nothing.

After Pasteur heated the vegetable juice, he let it sit in his long-necked flask. No animalcules appeared. So he let the juice sit some more. He let it sit for months. Still no animalcules were found in the juice. But some were found at the bottom of the curved part of the neck! This proved once and for all that the animalcules weren't spontaneously generated by the vegetable juice; they came from outside the flask.

That little curve in the neck of Pasteur's flask ended hundreds of years of scientific debate about—and thousands of years of widespread acceptance of—spontaneous generation.

Now scientists agree that living things don't come from dead things; they come from other living things of the same kind. With some animals only one parent is needed to make an offspring. A flatworm can make another flatworm just by splitting in two. With other animals two parents are needed to make an offspring. A male mouse supplies a sperm that fertilizes a female mouse's egg to make a new mouse. Worms and mice may be attracted to dirt, wheat, or vegetable juice. But these materials are never their parents. Their parents are other worms and mice.

So why do all those worms show up in your garbage? While flies are feasting on the bits of food you've thrown away, they drop off their eggs. When the eggs hatch, maggots—baby flies that look like worms—crawl out and feed on the garbage just as their parents did. Garbage makes a great nest for flies. But garbage doesn't give birth to baby flies any more than a bird's nest gives birth to chicks.

Rats appear in wheat-covered shirts for the same reason flies appear in garbage. They come to munch! But shirts and wheat don't give birth to rats any more than tables and pizza give birth to teenagers.

Can you explain the ants on a piece of candy, or the live flies around honey-covered dead flies? How do you suppose the idea of lambs coming from melons ever got started? Or geese coming from trees? Or frogs in a puddle coming from rain clouds? What controlled experiments could you set up to test your answers?

The "animalcules" found in vegetable juice are the tiny creatures we now call bacteria. As Pasteur suspected, they floated into Needham's flask from the air, on particles of dust. It doesn't take long for bacteria to reproduce; one bacterium just

TODAY'S SPECIAL:
VEGETABLE
JUICE

splits in two. So when a few bacteria wind up someplace where there's lots of food, a huge population can grow in no time. A flask filled with juice might be a great bacteria cafeteria. But vegetable juice doesn't give birth to bacteria; only bacteria can make more bacteria.

If spontaneous generation is impossible, why did scientists keep "proving" it was possible? Because it seemed so obvious that it was! They saw pieces of food teeming with creepy creatures when there were no other creatures anywhere else in the area, and felt *positive* that the creatures came from the food. These scientists believed in spontaneous generation so deeply that they couldn't step back from their belief to really test it. So they didn't consider other ways to explain the creatures' presence, or plan controlled experiments that would take other possible causes into account. Scientists have to examine their theories carefully and thoroughly—even parts that seem obviously right— if they want to come up with truths instead of goofs!

But the theory of spontaneous generation might not have been far from the truth in at least one way. Most scientists

38

today believe that the first living things on Earth did come from things that weren't living. They didn't spring to life quickly, by spontaneous generation. But very slowly, over hundreds of millions of years, certain chemicals did become tiny, simple living things . . . which evolved into all the creatures that now cover Earth!

So if a pair of giant extraterrestrials were looking down at the ball of Earth as it swirled by their noses for the first time in a billion years (a pretty short time for these giants), one giant might say to the other, "Yeech! Check out at all those weird, creepy creatures that have sprung to life on Earth. That little ball is swarming with them, but there aren't any to be seen anywhere else. . . . I thought you said there was no such thing as spontaneous generation!"

Burning to Know

What can grow from an inch to a yard in a second, and then shrink back down to nothing? What can cook your dinner, destroy your house, or blast you off into space? What can stand for hate, love, death, life, danger, power, or things that last forever? Nothing in the world can do all these things, except that amazing stuff called fire.

The ancients worshiped fire. They saw it leaping from the mouths of volcanoes, blasting through forests, and blazing on the face of the sun, and were in awe of its tremendous power.

Excuse me,
I ordered
medium rare.

When they learned to tap into that power by making fire themselves, their lives were transformed. Suddenly they could keep warm in the dead of winter. They could roast raw meats till they were tender, harden clay into pottery, craft mighty weapons and sturdy sculptures, and light up the pitch-darkness of a moonless night. No wonder they thought fire was a gift from the gods.

Saying that fire comes from the gods isn't a very scientific way of explaining its presence. But how much better could you do?

Stare at the fire in a fireplace and try to explain what's causing those bouncing orange stripes of flame. Something on the bark of the logs? Something inside the logs? If so, how come it only causes flames to leap from logs at certain times? And how come when you look at a cross-section of a log, you don't see anything but wood? But if the flames aren't caused by something on or in the wood, what else could possibly be causing them? What else is there in the fireplace?

Warming your hands by the fire is relaxing . . . but trying to figure out how fire happens could drive you nuts! That's why the ancients were happy to make use of fire's warmth and light, and make up stories to explain its presence.

The scientific approach to solving the mystery of fire had to wait until the late 1600s. That's when

German scientist G. E. Stahl came up with a theory that fire is caused by invisible stuff he called "phlogiston." According to Stahl, whenever something burned, it was giving off phlogiston; flames were really bursts of burning phlogiston.

Great fireplace logs—chockful o phlogiston!

Although Stahl didn't know what phlogiston was or what it was made of, he had ideas about what it did. For one thing, he believed phlogiston could flow in and out of things. Something that had absorbed a lot of phlogiston would burn rapidly, but something that was drained of phlogiston wouldn't burn at all. He also decided that phlogiston must be made of very tiny particles. They had to be tiny, since phlogiston seemed able to fit into tiny things; even the smallest splinter of wood can burn.

At first the phlogiston theory fit perfectly with everything people observed. As logs burn, they get smaller. As paper burns, it crinkles up and gets smaller too. And in both cases, the burning objects tend to give off smoke. These things helped convince people that fire is caused by something that leaves burning objects.

Another thing that supported the phlogiston theory is the way you can put out a fire by smothering it—like when you cover a flickering candle with a cup, or blast a small flame with the powder from a fire extinguisher. If an object needs to give off phlogiston to burn, then of course it would have trouble burning when it was covered up—there'd be no place for the phlogiston to go!

But then the phlogiston theory hit a major bump. Scientists noticed that when they burned metals, the metals didn't crinkle up or get smaller in any way. In fact, they got heavier! How could an object give something off and get heavier?

This observation forced Stahl's theory into a corner. But rather than give up on it, he made a desperate attempt to rescue his theory by drawing this bizarre conclusion: Phlogiston has negative weight.

Huh? Negative weight? Weight a minute!

Think about the idea of negative weight. Something with negative weight weighs less than zero pounds. (No weigh!) If coins had negative weight, when you put them in your pocket, you'd get lighter. If you took a few out, you'd get heavier. If you stuffed your pockets with enough of these crazy coins, you'd float away!

A helium balloon can float away because it's lighter than air. But even things that are lighter than air are still heavier than nothing. If there was no air in a room, the helium balloon would sink right to the ground. To this day we haven't found anything that weighs less than nothing.

Even in Stahl's day the idea of negative weight seemed pretty farfetched. But no one had a better idea, so people kept on accepting the phlogiston theory for almost a century, until a new discovery opened the door to a better one.

In the late 1700s scientists discovered that air isn't a single, pure gas, but a bunch of different gases all mixed together. When they started a fire in one of the gases, the fire burned even more brightly than in regular air. They called this gas "dephlogisticated air," since it seemed eager to take in phlogiston (in the same way that people call you "dehydrated" when you're eager to take in water).

When they tried to start a fire in another of the gases, nothing happened. So they called this gas "phlogisticated

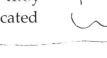

air," because it seemed to be already filled with all the phlogiston it could take.

The discovery that fire burns differently in different kinds of air could be explained in terms of the phlogiston theory. But a startling discovery made in one of these kinds of air led to a whole new theory . . . and phlogiston's phinish!

When Antoine Lavoisier burned metal in dephlogisticated air, which he called oxygen, he found that the metal did indeed gain weight—and the amount of oxygen decreased! This convinced Lavoisier that something burns not because it gives off phlogiston, but because it takes in oxygen.

We now know that Lavoisier was right—and that Stahl had it exactly backward. An object doesn't have to be filled with anything to burn. It does have to be surrounded by something: oxygen. This is true for a fire wherever it happens—in a forest, in a volcano, in your fireplace, or on your marshmallow.

Then why does a burning log get smaller? Because as burning wood combines with oxygen from the air, it turns to ash. The smoke given off is also a result of wood combining with oxygen—not some mysterious substance inside the wood.

You can put out a fire by smothering it because fire needs oxygen to survive, just as you do. That's why you can't start a fire in "phlogisticated" air—nitrogen—or in any gas other than oxygen.

So there's no such thing as phlogiston. It was a phiction, a phunny phantasy, a gooph! That weird invisible stuff with negative weight never flowed in or out of anything—except the minds of millions of people.

But for something that never existed, phlogiston sure played an important role in our lives! By putting forth his theory about phlogiston, Stahl got people trying to explain fire—not with fables and myths, but by observing, studying, and measuring. Eventually Stahl's imaginative wrong answer pointed scientists in the right direction . . . to the secret they were burning to know.

For the Birds

Have you ever watched a bird sail through the clouds and wished you could do the same? People have longed to fly like birds since the dawn of time.

Some have satisfied their longing by making up stories about superheroes who can fly, such as the ancient Greek gods or the comic-book heroes of today. Others have been contented to read about these characters, or paint pictures of them, or dress up like them at Halloween . . . or close their eyes and imagine that they too can fly like birds.

But there have also been people who weren't content to imagine flying. They had to try to figure out how to do it themselves.

Unlike many other scientific quests, this one wasn't primarily undertaken with any practical purpose in mind. Those who searched for the secret to flight didn't do it to cure diseases, build metals, or discover routes. They did it to satisfy their dreams.

Many of the first would-be flyers were tower jumpers. That's right, they strapped feathers or other materials to their arms and leapt from high towers.

Hey, it works for me!

ACME FLYING SUIT

They must have looked idiotic to anyone who watched them, flapping frantically as they plunged. But in some ways these laughable leaps seemed worth the risk. After all, people had learned to paddle like ducks and swing through the trees like monkeys so easily. Birds make flying from a high branch look like the simplest stunt of all!

One of the first tower jumpers was the Chinese emperor Shun. Three thousand years ago he jumped from a tower dressed as a bird, with wings attached to his hat. Though there's no record of the injuries Shun suffered, there are plenty of accounts of other flappers' flops. One tower jumper sailed right into the side of a church.

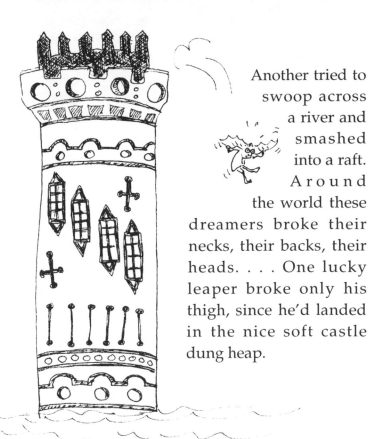

Another tried to swoop across a river and smashed into a raft. Around the world these dreamers broke their necks, their backs, their heads. . . . One lucky leaper broke only his thigh, since he'd landed in the nice soft castle dung heap.

In the 1800s people discovered why all tower jumpers were doomed to dropping. Close study of birds' bodies revealed that there was a lot more to a bird than flapping feathers. For one thing, there was tremendous muscle. When compared to the weight of its tiny body, a bird's chest muscles are incredibly powerful. If birds were the size of humans, they'd be eight times as strong. They could thwack us to bits!

Close study also revealed that a bird's wings power its flight in two different ways. For one, they provide lift, the force that lifts up a bird as it sails. This force is aided by the wing's shape—flat on the bottom and curved on top.

For another, a bird's wings provide thrust, the force that thrusts a bird ahead. To use this force the fingerlike tips of the wings' feathers grip the wind and twist, yanking the bird forward.

The discovery of birds' superior chest muscles made one thing perfectly clear: Humans could never do what birds do with our mere bodies. People who wanted to fly would have to build some kind of machine that could lift them up and carry them away. And the discovery of the forces a bird's wings provide gave clues about how to construct these machines. To provide lift for their flying machines, people used long flat planes that were curved on top. To thrust their planes forward, they used propellers that would grip the wind as they twirled.

The people who built these machines and intended to make them fly were more scientific than tower jumpers. But in the eyes of the public, they too were a bunch of doomed lunatics. Everyone loved to laugh at these daredevils, whom they considered far more suited for the circus than for the science lab. And sometimes the would-be flyers actually  behaved like circus performers; to raise money to pay for their machines, they would try them out in front of huge, whooping, jeering, cheering, sneering—and paying—crowds.

If the audience came to see disaster, they were rarely disappointed. The first flying machines were huge gliders that sailed recklessly across fields and came crashing down at the slightest shift in the wind.

With the invention of the steam engine, flyers finally had a source of power that might drive their machines through the wind. But a steam engine is a large, heavy metal furnace. While it provided power, it had to use a lot of its power just to lift itself off the ground.

To lift these bulky burners, many steam-powered flying machines were built with two pairs of wings—or more. One had so many wings, it looked like a gigantic set of venetian blinds on wheels!

But whether they had two wings or twenty, the steam-powered flying machines proved too weak to take off or too heavy to stand more than a second

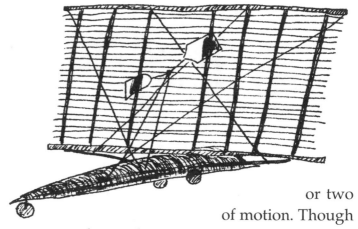

or two of motion. Though these planes were terrible at flying, they were great at flying apart—and entertaining a jeering crowd.

Some flyers turned to other sources of power to get their dream machines off the ground. They built planes powered by batteries, rubber bands, and even clockwork. These sources of power are strong enough to work your flashlight, your toy glider, or your wristwatch. But they proved too weak to send people soaring through the sky.

When cars were invented, most people couldn't wait to go driving down the road. But the flyers couldn't wait to go driving up into the sky—with the help of the incredible new gasoline engine that gave cars their power. It was light. It was powerful. It was only a matter of time!

The race was on to see who would be the first human being to make a gasoline-powered flight. Every last, desperate step toward the finish line of this race was filled with flops. But every flop led to new knowledge that others gained from—even if the knowledge was simply: "Don't try what I just tried!"

It certainly wasn't hard to flop. Look at all those propellers, planks, flaps, wires, and wheels. One tiny error in how the plane was built could cause the plane to lurch, tip, rip, flip, tumble, roll, or fall apart into a hundred pieces—before ever leaving the ground.

But even if a plane was perfectly built, its flight wasn't goof-proof. Skill in working the plane was just as important—and harder to get. When you ride a bicycle or drive a car, you have only two directions to consider: left and right. But flyers had four directions to worry about: left, right, up, and down. And they didn't have much time to make decisions. The slightest delay could make them crash.

Super flying skills is what set American flyers Orville and Wilbur Wright apart. The Wright Brothers built a plane that required even more control than other planes. Instead of sitting up in their plane, the driver had to lie on his belly as he worked many controls.

With this plane, even more than others, driving skill would make the difference between flight and goof. So the Wright Brothers practiced. For four and a half years they practiced flying gliders through a wind tunnel, making hundreds of test flights a month.

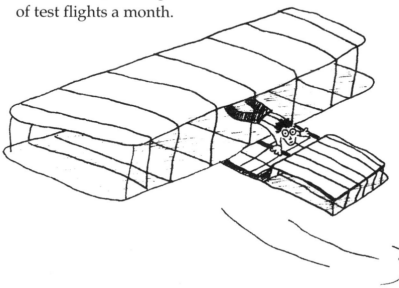

When they finally felt ready, they tried out their gasoline-powered plane on the beaches of North Carolina. Their first try failed. So did their second. Time and again, both plane and pilot went crashing into the sand. But with careful adjustments, the Wright Brothers eventually made it into the air, and into the history

books. They achieved the first controlled, powered flight—of 40 yards. One short flight for a bird; one giant flight for a human!

So now people could fly. But there were many goofs ahead on the path to flying safely. Orville Wright himself came crashing to the ground when the propeller of his plane stuck in one of its wires. Though he survived with a few broken ribs, his passenger broke his skull and died.

But as people kept goofing, they kept learning from their goofs. They created better and better flying machines . . . and eventually came up with the modern jet plane, which can go faster than the speed of sound.

Look at the drawing of the plane of today. We sure have come a long way from feathered arms and winged caps! But all of the tower jumpers, and all the people with their flying machines, took the same basic approach to flying that designers of the modern plane did. They all imitated birds.

The plane's streamlined shape is modeled after a bird's. Its long, broad wings with their curved tops are shaped like a bird's. The plane's metallic tail even resembles a bird's tail feathers. And just as the bird has its tremendously powerful chest muscles, the plane has a tremendous source of power in its jet engine.

Those dreamers who jumped out of towers flapping their arms were easy to laugh at; so were the ones who tried to take off in ridiculous collapsing contraptions. They were mocked. Their bones were broken. And often, in their gloriously goofy quest, they died. But their dream never died.

Thanks to those dreamers, you can sit back and take off into the clouds. You can feel yourself being thrust forward and lifted up. You can gaze down over highways, rivers, open fields, and oceans. You can soar through the air. You can fly.

Bars on Mars!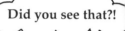

T hey're out there! Just look at the night sky!
Blinking dots. Flashing streaks. Shifting shadows. Bursts of color in the haze. The harder you
strain your eyes, the more certain you
become: They're out there. They're
active. They're alive.

Did you see that?!

Have you ever looked into the night sky and seen clues of life on other planets? Back when people thought Earth was the center of the universe, they also figured it was the only planet with living beings. After all, the other planets were just a bunch of shiny ornaments hung up there to delight the inhabitants of the one centrally located, all-important planet, Earth. But when people realized that the other planets in the solar system are just as important as Earth, they began to suspect there must be life on those planets too.

In particular, scientists wondered about Earth's neighbor Mars. The more they studied it, the more Mars seemed like Earth's twin. Mars has four seasons. Its day is only slightly longer than 24 hours. It has ice caps on its north and south poles, as Earth does. And if the huge dark splotches scientists observed on its surface were bodies of water, Mars too was covered with oceans. It seemed only logical that this planet, which had so much else in common with ours, must also have intelligent life.

Some scientists were so sure there was intelligent life on Mars, they started planning how to inform the intelligent creatures up there about the intelligent creatures down here. One scientist thought we should grow a huge wheat field in the shape of a triangle and surround it with pine trees so the Martians could see we know geometry. Another suggested digging a 20-mile ditch across the Sahara desert, filling it with kerosene, and lighting it to get the Martians' attention. A third suggested building a huge mirror across Europe and angling it carefully so we could use the sun's light to write an interplanetary greeting card on the Martian desert. While some scientists concentrated on giving the Martians clues about us, Italian astronomer

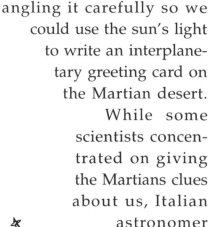

Giovanni
Schiaparelli
searched the sky
for clues about them.

One night about a hundred years ago, when Mars was passing close to Earth, Schiaparelli saw something on Mars that astounded him. Running between the ice caps on Mars's poles and the splotches thought to be oceans was a network of smooth, wide lines.

He'd seen planets covered with markings before—markings that were randomly scattered, as things made by nature tend to be. But there was nothing random about these markings. They were smooth, neat, and evenly spaced. Not one of them bent, or twisted, or stopped in the middle of nowhere—every single marking connected an ice cap to an ocean.

In announcing his findings, Schiaparelli wrote that he'd seen forty channels on Mars. Channels are narrow rivers made by nature. But the Italian word for channels is *canali*, which suggested to English-speaking readers that Schiaparelli was talking about canals. Canals are a lot like channels, except for one important thing: Canals aren't made by nature. They're made by living beings. Schiaparelli himself liked this idea. It seemed likely to him that the *canali* were in fact canals, built to transport water from Mars's polar ice caps and oceans to its desserts.

To get an idea what a big deal canals were to people in those days, consider what a big deal hi-tech equipment is to us today. We measure our progress by the quality of our computers, CD players, satellites, microwave ovens, and video games. In those days people proudly measured their progress by their canals. They'd just built the historic Suez Canal, digging through a hundred miles of land to join the Mediterranean and Red Seas. And they were about to start building the Panama Canal, which would join the Atlantic and Pacific Oceans. (No more sailing all the way around South America to get from New York to California!) Their ability to build these incredible canals made people feel like masters of their planet. Since scientists were searching for intelligent life, and canals were the measure of a civilization's intelligence, the idea of canals on Mars made sense to many scientists— and thrilled them.

One who was especially thrilled was American astronomer Percival Lowell. Even before he heard about Schiaparelli's canali, he believed there was intelligent life on Mars. Though many others who looked for the canals didn't see them, Lowell did. He used bigger and bigger telescopes to study the surface of Mars, until he saw not forty but hundreds of canals.

Since these Martian canals looked much larger than those on Earth, and since there were so many more up there than down here, Lowell decided Martian civilization must be far more advanced than our own. He agreed with Schiaparelli that the canals were used to carry water from the polar ice caps. But Lowell felt the dark splotches to which the canals led weren't oceans; they were towns where Martians lived on huge farms irrigated by the canals.

Why were Martians going to so much trouble to get the water to these farms? Lowell reasoned that if Martian civilization was more advanced than ours, Martians had probably been on Mars longer than we'd been on Earth. In fact, Martians had probably been around for so

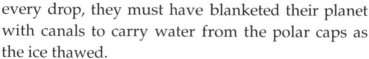

long that they'd used up most of their water. Desperate for every drop, they must have blanketed their planet with canals to carry water from the polar caps as the ice thawed.

And these weren't the only conclusions Lowell drew about the Martians. When other scientists announced that there must not be much air on Mars, Lowell countered by suggesting that these Martians might not have lungs at all, but gills!

The idea of intelligent Martians with gills enchanted intelligent Earthlings with lungs. Telescope sales soared.

Everybody wanted to get a peek at the amazing network of canals made by their thirsty space neighbors.

Some people saw Lowell's wide stripes. Others saw a pattern that looked more like a spiderweb. But many couldn't see the canals at all. And over the years, as telescopes became more powerful, fewer and fewer people saw the canals.

Then, in the 1970s, close-up photos of Mars taken by American and Soviet spacecraft brought all wondering about the canali to a finale. The photos showed that the splotches Schiaparelli thought were oceans and Lowell thought were Martians were just a certain kind of rock. And where the astronomers had seen canals, the photos revealed—nothing! Not even a trace of the *canali!* Oops. Stargazers Schiaparelli and Lowell had pulled a stellar goof.

Though the photos didn't reveal canals, they did show scattered narrow lines on Mars, as well as shifting clouds of dust swirling across the Martian surface. Maybe people viewing these scattered shapes from millions of miles away found them uncannily canaly. Or maybe the optical illusion was caused entirely by the scientists' own eyes, as they squinted and strained to see in the darkness.

But these goofed viewings of Mars were more than optical illusions. They were mental illusions—fantasies.

Have you ever looked up at clouds and seen faces of people or creatures that have been on your mind recently? Canals and intelligent life on Mars were on Schiaparelli's and Lowell's minds.

So as they gazed through telescopes, their impressions were shaped by their imaginations. They saw simple patterns of light and imagined a race of superior beings who built canals, as people today see lights in the night and imagine a race of superior beings who build hi-tech spacecraft.

So the pair of scientists who saw canals on Mars were double goofers; they goofed with their eyes and with their minds. But apart from their Martian misunderstanding, they weren't goofy—they were great. Schiaparelli made important discoveries about Venus, and Lowell made observations that led to the discovery of Pluto.

Schiaparelli and Lowell were smart, precise, hardworking, widely respected, successful astronomers. And unlike many other scientific goofers, these two were completely committed to the importance of observation. But even when you think you're relying on direct observation, what you hope to see can get in the way of what you do see.

Today scientists search for intelligent life far beyond our solar system. Using an array of extraordinary devices, they check billions of miles out into space for signals that might be messages from a distant civilization.

If these scientists pick up a signal, you can be sure they test it carefully to make sure they're not just seeing what they want to see. Because even funnier than a race of canal builders with gills or robots with ray guns is a race of beings who spend their lives searching for the truth, completely unaware that their eyes are ruled by their imaginations.

Charge, Spot!

W hat's wrong with this
picture of the Goofbergs'
living room? The television doesn't
have an antenna? That's okay, the
Goofbergs have cable. The com-
puter isn't hooked up to a printer?
That's okay, they take their disks to Granny
Goofberg, who has a laser jet. What's wrong with
this picture is: The electronic devices are all plugged
into animals. As silly as it seems, this really could
happen—according to a theory, once widely respected, about a weird, wacky source of electricity.

People have known about electricity since the dawn of history. The ancients knew they could rub stones together to create electric sparks. They also knew electricity passed through certain materials more easily than others.

One thing you know about electricity is that it can pass through humans. If you don't believe it, rub your feet on a carpet and touch a metal door-knob, for a lesson that might shock you. But you also know something about electricity the ancients never imagined. You know people can control electricity to power lights, cameras, action toys, and hundreds of other things you use every day. As recently as three centuries ago, people had no idea that electricity could be used to do things, till a certain discovery got them all charged up.

As Luigi Galvani began his laboratory demonstration one day, the last thing he wanted to do was make a historic discovery about electricity. After all, Galvani was a doctor! His lesson wasn't about electricity. It was about what happens to the nerves in a frog's leg when they're pressed.

But when Galvani's assistant touched the frog's nerve with a metal scalpel, the leg shook, twitched, and kicked. No, this wasn't happening because the frog was ticklish—the frog was dead. Deceased. It had croaked. And yet there was that leg doing a frenzied polka. Could it be, Galvani wondered, that the scalpel had tapped into a source of electricity inside the frog?

Though electricity wasn't Galvani's field, he was a careful scientist. So he went home to test his hunch in different controlled situations.

He attached the frog's leg to his iron fence with a copper hook. Again the mysterious electrical source went to work: Each time the leg touched the fence, it twitched.

Might the electricity be coming from the sky? Galvani wondered. After all, Ben Franklin had shown that electricity can cruise through the sky in the form of lightning. So Galvani took the frog into his house and attached it to a metal plate. Though hidden from the sky, the frog still hadn't been separated from the source of electricity: Again the leg twitched.

Might the electricity be coming from the air in the room? he considered. To answer this question, Galvani placed the frog in a closed container and sucked out all of the air. Again the leg twitched when it touched the metal plate. Where could the electricity possibly be coming from? It must be coming from the muscles in the frog's leg!

There was only one version of the experiment in which the frog's leg didn't twitch: when Galvani attached the leg to glass instead of metal. So he decided that metal was crucial, because it let the electricity flow out from the frog.

The results of these experiments seemed to Galvani to fit together perfectly. So he announced his theory of animal electricity: Electricity comes from the muscles and nerves of animals.

Though it might sound strange to you, Galvani's theory made sense to a lot of people. They'd already experienced animal electricity first-hand—or first foot, by stepping on an electric eel and getting a powerful electric shock. When other scientists repeated Galvani's frog experiments and got the same results, they too were convinced.

Go ahead, make my day!

But then one scientist decided to try Galvani's experiment with a twist. Alessandro Volta figured that if Galvani was right, it shouldn't matter whether the frog's leg was touching two pieces of different metals—like Galvani's iron fence and copper hook—or just one piece of metal. After all, the metals were just there to carry the electricity that came from the frog.

When Volta attached a piece of copper and a piece of zinc to the frog's leg, the leg did the same kind of berserk breakdance it had done for Galvani. But when Volta connected two ends of a single metal wire to a frog's leg, the leg hardly moved. Aha, Volta thought, these bursts of movement might be caused by the metals, not the frog.

Then Volta removed the frog from the experiment completely. He placed copper and zinc in salt water, connected them by a wire, and found that a strong electric current flowed between them. Galvani had goofed! And Volta had done more than prove that electricity comes from metals instead of animals. He'd made the first battery!

We now know that electricity is the flow of tiny particles called electrons. The metals Galvani used caused bursts of electricity, because metals give off electrons more easily than other elements do. It matters which metal is used, since some metals give off electrons more easily than others. It also matters if more than one metal is used, since one metal that gives off electrons especially easily can pass its electrons to another metal that draws electrons in, causing a faster flow of electrons—and a

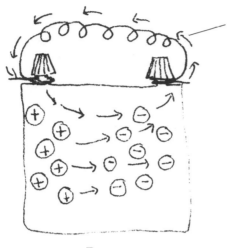

Attach the battery to your lamp, and the electricity traveling through will light your room.

Electrons travel across from one metal to another.

Battery

more powerful burst of electricity. In a battery, metals are carefully arranged so electrons will flow from one metal to another for a long time, providing lots of power.

Though powerful bursts of electricity can flow through animals' nerves and muscles, causing their limbs to shake, these bursts don't come from the animals' nerves and muscles. When scientists studied the few animals that give shocks, like electric eels and stingrays, they found that these creatures have special electrical organs that allow them to stun attackers and electrocute prey. But even in these cases, the animal electricity doesn't come from inside nerves or muscles.

So Galvani goofed. But by bringing metals together to receive animal electricity, he inspired

Volta to bring metals together to create the first battery. Galvani's scalpel did more than make a frog's leg twitch; it lighted up the world with electric power. That's why Galvani's name gives us the word "galvanize," which means to inspire action. Galvani's goof galvanized the globe!

Make a Monkey

Yay ou've just made an incredible discovery. After hearing that the remains of a prehistoric beast might be buried somewhere in your neighborhood, you went digging through the snow in your back-

yard and found: a weird green hunk.

You're dying to know what the creature who owned this hunk looked like. So based on this single creature piece, you imagine the whole creature picture. Maybe you decide the hunk was a toe, or a nose, or a bump on the end of its tail. Or maybe you suppose the creature was so huge that this hunk was once a single taste bud on its titanic tongue.

Building a model from only a single piece can be revealing. But in this case it would be embarrassing. As the hunk thawed out, you'd realize by its garlicky smell that it's not a prehistoric snout, but a modern-day pickle. Oops.

In the late 1800s, scientists were trying to piece together a model of a relative of theirs, and yours: the earliest human being. According to Darwin's new theory of evolution, humans didn't suddenly appear on Earth looking just as we do today, but evolved from some type of prehistoric creature. So scientists everywhere were searching for bones that might have belonged to our prehistoric parents.

Though people around the world were eager to find out what the first humans looked like, the English were more eager than most. Bones had been found that belonged to a prehistoric German—the flat-topped, big-browed Neanderthal man. And bones had been found that belonged to a prehistoric Frenchman—the less brutish Cro-Magnon man. These discoveries made the English desperate to find a prehistoric ancestor on their own soil.

Why was it such a big deal to the English? Because at that time England was the most powerful country in the world. With its mighty British Empire, England ruled colonies all around the world. The English boldly spread their way of life around the globe because they felt they were special. Part of what they felt made them special was their English blood—the simple fact that they were descended from other English people. So they found the idea that their ancestors may have been from other, second-rate countries alarming.

As English scientists searched their land for a prehistoric Englishman that was older—and, if possible, handsomer—than any human ancestor yet found, the evidence they sought was waiting deep in a muddy pit.

Englishman Charles Dawson wasn't a professional scientist; he studied rocks as a hobby. One day as he passed a farm in Piltdown, Dawson noticed in a pit by the road a certain kind of flint that wasn't usually found that far north. Since scientists had discovered prehistoric tools made from this rock, Dawson thought this spot just might have been an ancient toolmaking site. So he told the farmhands to be on the lookout for bones.

A few years later a worker stuck his pickax into what seemed like a coconut. But coconuts don't grow in England. When Dawson was summoned, he saw at once that it definitely was not a coconut.

It was the top of a mysterious human skull that had blackened with age.

Dawson showed the skull fragment to a professional scientist friend who shared Dawson's curiosity. Together they returned to the pit to search for more parts of this possibly prehistoric person.

Thinking about their ancestor was inspiring; digging for their ancestor was grueling. The pit was filled with layer upon layer of sand, clay, rock, and muck. And they couldn't just dig through it with a shovel. After all, the evidence they sought might be as tiny as a tooth. They had to go through the slime a handful at a time, passing every bit through a sieve. But these two were driven.

They devoted their weekends, vacations, and every free minute to the torturous task.

Why yuck, old man.

'Tis a tad slimy, indeed.

And suddenly all the work proved worthwhile. On three days in a row the muddy duo found three more parts of the same skull. Then, in almost the same spot, they found the strangest thing yet: a chunk of a jaw that had a few teeth.

There was something strange about this jaw, all right. Though it looked a lot like an ape's jaw, the teeth were flat, like human teeth. With prehistoric bones scattered so sparsely around the globe, the odds of unrelated fossils showing up right next to each other seemed tiny. And all of the pieces were the same color—they appeared to be the same age! So even though the jaw seemed more apelike than the rest of the skull, the two felt sure these parts belonged together.

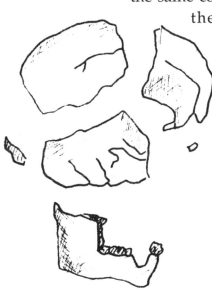

Pieces of Piltdown Man

So they got right to work building a model. Putting together this model was a lot tougher than putting together a model you might buy in a box. Most of the pieces were missing. And there was no picture on a box cover to show them what they were aiming for. They had to guess what the missing pieces would look like, guess how the bones fit together, estimate how much room would be needed for the tongue and brain . . .

The creature they came up with was slightly apelike, but they thought it was better looking than Neanderthal man and Cro-Magnon man. This ancient creature appeared more intelligent, more graceful, more dignified . . . more English!

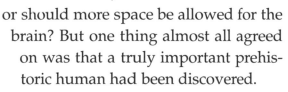

When Piltdown man was presented to a panel of British experts, they had lots of questions. Was he 100,000 years old or two million? Was the shape of the model correct, or should more space be allowed for the brain? But one thing almost all agreed on was that a truly important prehistoric human had been discovered.

When the story hit the newspapers, Piltdown man became an instant celebrity. Across the country he was hailed as the oldest Englishman, if not the parent of all humanity. People across the nation rushed to buy souvenir models of their handsome ancestor.

But by the 1950s the Piltdown passion had died down. One after another, England's colonies had won their independence; the days of the British Empire were over. Now English scientists were less worried about finding the earliest Englishman and more interested in working with scientists around the world to find the earliest humans. And they were becoming more and more confused about Piltdown man's role in the story.

Piltdown man was different from the other early humans that had been found. The others all fit into a group of apelike primates that became more human as time went by. Piltdown man didn't fit in this group.

So scientists began to take closer looks at the pieces from Piltdown. One of these closer looks revealed something extremely suspicious: fine scratch marks on the tips of Piltdown man's teeth.

It's not unusual for teeth to be worn away by eating. As you eat, different teeth wear down at different rates, depending on where you do most of your chewing.

But Piltdown man's teeth had all been worn down in the exact same way. When teeth wear away like that, it isn't caused by eating. It isn't caused by decay. It's caused by filing. Someone had taken a file to those teeth! But why?

By applying various chemicals to Piltdown man's bones, scientists discovered that the skull and jaw had been stained so they looked like they belonged together. Next, new methods of testing revealed that the skull wasn't prehistoric. It was only a few hundred years old. And the jaw wasn't even as old as that—or human. It belonged to a modern-day orangutan whose teeth had been filed to make them look human. Oops. Dawson had goofed.

But *this* scientific goof was caused by a scientific spoof. How could such a thing happen? Did someone plant the bones in the pit to prove the first humans were English? Did someone plant them to make Dawson look like an idiot? Did Dawson plant them there himself? To this day no one knows who was responsible for the Piltdown hoax that fooled so many experts for so long.

A few decades after Piltdown man was shown to be a fake, scientists have come a lot closer to finding our common human ancestor. Scientists today believe that the earliest human ancestor lived in East Africa two million years ago. She doesn't look much like Piltdown man. But she owes him a debt, as do all our models of prehistoric creatures.

Piltdown man taught scientists to be extremely careful when they make models from fossils. He inspired scientists to develop better ways to find out how old a fossil is. And he reminded people in all sciences to be on the lookout not only for accidental errors, but also for fraud. Not bad for someone who never lived.

It's easy to laugh at the way Dawson pulled an orangutan's jaw out of the mud and decided he'd found his ancestor. But when you get right down to it, that's how scientists have come up with everything we know today about prehistoric life.

I owe it all to Piltdown man.

Dinosaurs lived millions of years ago. Their remains are few and far between. So scientists have to put together puzzles with most of the pieces missing. They try to figure out how the bones fit together, what the flesh that covered them looked like, how their owners moved and defended themselves, and what they liked to eat by looking at fossils and comparing them to creatures that roam Earth today.

But as they draw these conclusions, scientists are careful to test them, examine their results closely, and invite others to do the same . . . so that their fossils don't make monkeys of them!

Goof Forth
and Prosper

You're swirling through space on a rock covered with blobs—and you're totally flabbergasted. That blob you bit just bit you back! You have no idea what's edible. What's animal. What's up. What's down. What's going on!

You stagger and stumble and bobble till you bump into—people! Mobs of people. Some are stumbling. Some are bobbling. But most aren't bobbling at all. They're moving among the blobs with ease. They're using the blobs to do incredible things!

These people have been on the rock a lot longer than you. They've been bumbling and bungling and goofing for years. And they've learned a ton from their goofs.

They've learned how to use the blobs for food, warmth, transportation, and medicine. They've studied the slabs you're standing on to map out the entire rock. They've studied the gobs in the sky to figure out where your rock has been and where it's going. They've even figured out how to rub blobs against slabs to tap into the power of the gobs!

But the more they know about life on the rock, the more they know they don't know. They have no idea what's inside the tiniest blobs.

Or what's beyond the largest gobs. Or what the power of the gobs is doing inside the slabs. There are forces to tame. Diseases to cure. Countless new questions to answer.

These people are burning for new answers. They're close to new answers. But they just can't get them. To get new answers, they need a new approach. A new idea. A new mind. They need: you.

How can you help solve the mysteries of life on this rock? First you need to study what the others have learned. The methods they've used. The answers they've found.

Respect these answers. Admire them. Learn how they're right. Then imagine how they might be wrong.

Why? Because all their highly respected answers were reached when previous highly respected answers were shown to be goofs. To come up with new answers, you need to ask yourself: Which of these highly respected answers are really scientific goofs?

You need to snoop for goofs.

So step back to study the highly respected answers from a distance. Turn your head sideways to examine the highly respected answers from a different angle. Stand on your head to see what the highly respected answers look like upside down.

Question the highly respected answers in every imaginable way. Might they be exactly backward, like the answers of Ptolemy, Stahl, and Galvani? Might they seem logical but be way off base, like the answers of Maria the alchemist and Emperor Shun? Might they be based on optical illusions or mental delusions, like the answers of Schiaparelli and Lowell? Might they be based on uncontrolled experiments, as Van Helmont's answer was? Might they be based on fudged evidence, as Columbus's answer was? Might they be based on fraud, like Dawson's? Might they might they might they . . .

Highly
Respected Dog

Your new questions will suggest new answers. Try them on. Try them out. Test them again and again.

If you proceed with intelligence, care, and imagination, you too may goof. Even the greatest of goof snoopers goof.

But you also may break through the roof. You may come up with amazing answers. Brilliant answers. Stunning answers that no one ever dreamed of. Swirling through a goofy universe, you just may goof to the truth.

Glossary / Index

D

Darwin, Charles 77. *English scientist who lived in the 1800s. He argued that humans evolved from a prehistoric creature.*

Dawson, Charles 78–81, 89. *Englishman who found the bones thought to be Piltdown man.*

dinosaurs 84–85. *Reptiles that lived millions of years ago. Scientists find out about them by studying fossils.*

double-boiling. See water bath.

E

Earth 8, 11–12, 21–22, 27–28
   theories about 6–7, 8–9, 11, 22, 23, 24, 25, 38–39, 59

electricity 69–75. *The flow of electrons.*

electrons 73–74. *Tiny particles that can flow from one metal to another to become electricity.*

elements 16, 18–19. *The basic materials from which matter is made; the building blocks of matter.*

Erastothenes 24. *Ancient Greek scientist who calculated Earth's size by measuring shadows.*

evolution 39, 76–85. *The way living things evolve, or develop and change, over time.*

exploration 21, 22–24, 27–29

F

fakes 17, 83, 84, 89

fire 40–46

flying 47–50, 56–57

flying machines 50–57

fossils 84–85. *Traces of a plant or animal that lived long ago, fixed firmly in Earth's crust.*

fudging 27, 89. *Adjusting observations to make them fit a scientific theory.*

G

Galvani, Luigi 70–75, 89. *Italian doctor who lived in the 1700s. He thought electricity comes from the muscles of animals.*

garbage. See spontaneous generation.

gold 14–18

gravity 8, 12. *The force that moves objects toward the ground and moves planets and stars around.*

I

Island of Earth, 22. *Medieval European name for Europe, Asia and Africa.*

K

kerotakis 15–17 (see also Maria). *Device designed to make gold by mixing another metal with vaporized liquid.*

Kircher, Athanasius 32, 33 (see also spontaneous generation). *German scientist who lived in the 1600s.*

L

Lavoisier, Antoine 45. *French chemist who lived in the 1700s. He discovered that things burn because they take in oxygen.*

lift 50. *The force that lifts up a bird in flight.*

Lowell, Percival 62–63, 64, 66. *Astronomer who lived in the United States in the late 1800s and early 1900s. He thought there were intelligent beings on Mars.*

M

Magellan, Ferdinand 27. *Portuguese explorer of the late 1500s and early 1600s who sailed west from Europe around the world.*

maps and globes 20, 21, 25, 27–29

Maria 14–19. *Alchemist who lived in Alexandria, Egypt, in the second century. She invented scientific methods still used today.*

Mars 8, 59–67

microscope 33–34

Milky Way Galaxy 12

model 76–77, 80–81, 83. *Copy of something, used by scientists to figure out how that thing works.*

moon 5–6, 8

N

nature 2. *Everything on Earth, and in the rest of the universe.*

Neanderthal man 77. *Prehistoric ancestor of humans, discovered in Germany.*

Needham, John 34–35, 37 (see also spontaneous generation). *English scientist who lived in the 1700s.*

negative weight 43–44, 46. *The theory that something can weigh less than nothing.*

nitrogen 45. *A gas that is part of the air.*

O

observation 6, 7, 12, 23, 27, 67–68. *Looking carefully at something.*

Ocean Sea 22. *Medieval European name for the oceans surrounding Europe, Asia, and Africa.*

oxygen 45. *A gas that is part of the air.*

P

Pasteur, Louis 35–36, 37. *French scientist who lived in the 1800s. He proved that the theory of spontaneous generation was wrong.*

phinish 45. *A way to spell "finish" when you're trying to be phunny.*

phlogiston 42–46 (see also Stahl, G. E.). *Substance that was thought to cause fire.*

Piltdown man 78–84. *Supposedly prehistoric ancestor of humans, found in England, that later was proven to be a fake.*

planets 8, 11, 12, 58–59, 67

  search for intelligent life on 59–60, 61, 62–68

Ptolemy 7, 8–10, 12, 14, 89. *Scientist who lived in Alexandria, Egypt, in the second century. He made a model that seemed to prove that the sun, moon, stars, and other planets revolved around Earth.*

R

Redi, Francesco 32–33 (see also spontaneous generation). *Italian scientist who lived in the 1600s.*

Renaissance 10, 17. *Period of European history from the 1300s through the 1600s when old ideas were questioned and new ideas were developed.*

reproduction 36–38 (see also spontaneous generation). *The way plants and animals make new plants and animals.*

S

Schiaparelli, Giovanni 60–61, 62, 66. *Italian astronomer who lived in the 1800s. He thought he discovered canals on Mars.*

science 2. *The way we try to understand or control nature.*

scientific experiments 8, 14, 15–17, 32, 39, 43, 45, 50–51, 71–73, 84–85, 89. *Tests done by scientists to prove or discover something.*

controlled 33, 34, 37, 38, 71. *Experiments in which only one part of a problem is tested at a time.*

scientific goofs 2–4, 12, 19, 27–28, 38, 46, 53, 56–57, 65, 67, 74–75, 83. *Scientific theories that prove to be wrong but can lead to scientific truths.*

scientific instruments 6, 15, 33, 34, 35–36, 67 (see also microscope; telescope). *Tools used by scientists.*

scientific method 15, 19, 26, 46, 84–85, 87–90. *A way of finding answers to scientific questions that uses careful observation, organization, and experiments.*

scientific theories 8, 18, 26, 27, 31, 38–39, 41–43, 45, 46, 70–73, 79, 80, 84–85, 88–90. *Ideas used to explain nature.*

scientific truths 2–3, 38, 90. *Theories that are proven to be true and are accepted by everybody.*

Shun 48. *Chinese emperor who lived three thousand years ago. He tried to fly by jumping from a tower while wearing a hat with wings attached to it.*

Spallanzani, Lazzaro 34–35 (see also spontaneous generation). *Italian scientist who lived in the 1700s.*

spontaneous generation 30–39. *The theory that animals can come to life without any other live animal playing a part in the process.*

Stahl, G. E. 41–43, 44, 45, 46, 89. *German scientist who lived in the 1600s. He thought fire is caused by phlogiston.*

stars 5–6, 8, 12

sun 5–6, 7, 8, 11, 12, 40

T

teenagers 37. *Humans who feed on pizza.*

telescope 11, 60, 61, 62, 64–65, 67

tools. See scientific instruments

Toscanelli, Paolo 25. *Italian mapmaker who lived in the 1400s.*

U

universe 2, 6, 8, 12, 59, 90. *Everything that exists.*

Further Reading

For more on Ptolemy's work and other self-centered ideas about the universe:

Gay, Kathlyn. *Science in Ancient Greece*. New York: Franklin Watts, 1988.

For more about Maria the Alchemist and other historic women scientists:

*Alic, Margaret. *Hypatia's Heritage*. Boston, Massachusetts: Beacon Press, 1986.

For a thorough account of Christopher Columbus' not-so-scientific process:

Dodge, Stephen C. *Christopher Columbus and the First Voyages to the New World*. New York: Chelsea House Publishers, 1991.

For a few more ha-storic theories about how creatures reproduce, and many more facts about reproduction:

Avraham, Regina. *The Reproductive System*. New York: Chelsea House Publishers, 1991.

Maria, Stahl, and many who learned from their mixing mix-ups are featured in this story of the development of chemistry:

*Brock, William H. *The Norton History of Chemistry*. New York: W.W. Norton & Company, Inc., 1993.

For the story of the Wright Brothers' lives and times, and a photo of that famous first flight.

Haynes, Richard M. *The Wright Brothers, Pioneers in Change*. Englewood Cliffs, New Jersey: Silver Burdett Press, Inc., 1991.

*Adult books

For the history of our understanding of Mars, from first fantasies to hi-tech NASA studies:

*Wilford, John Noble. *Mars Beckons*. New York: Alfred A. Knopf, 1990.

For more about electricity, including.a few ways it is generated—in small quantities—by the human body:

Vogt, Gregory. *Generating Electricity*. New York: Franklin Watts, 1986.

To learn about those wiggly water creatures who can zap you with bursts of electricity:

Halton, Cheryl Mays. *Those Amazing Eels*. Minneapolis, Minnesota: Dillon Press, 1990.

If you want to get better acquainted with your prehuman ancestors, this book is filled with photos of their bones and other things they left behind:

Eyewitness Books: *Early Humans*. London: Dorling Kindersley Limited. New York: Alfred A. Knopf, Inc., 1989

For more about the Piltdown spoof, including a few ideas about who might have done the spoofing:

*Spencer, Frank. *Piltdown, A Scientific Forgery*. London: British Museum of Natural History Publications. New York: Oxford University Press, 1990.

Another Book by the Author of
Scientific Goofs

They Came From DNA
by Billy Aronson
illustrations by Danny O'Leary

Skreeg 402 has been beamed down to Earth to study its creatures. How are Earth creatures made? What makes them so different from one another? How did they get this way?

Take a peek into a remarkable journal, and see how an alien discovers the secret: *They Came From DNA.*

"Fast paced, theatrical, tongue in cheek, . . . a winner."
—*Kirkus Reviews*

"Imaginative humor."
—*The Wall Street Journal*

"Delightful tale of science fact."
—*Odyssey Magazine*

"Entertaining introduction to genetics."
—*Booklist*

"A lighthearted romp with serious factual foundations. . . . A sparkling approach to the scientific method."
—*Science & Children*